Inglés sin Barreras.

El Video-Maestro de Inglés Conversacional

8 La salud

Cuaderno de ejercicios

Para información sobre
Inglés sin Barreras
en oferta especial de
Referido Preferido
1-800-305-6472
Dé el Código 03429

ISBN: 1-59172-310-8

I704WB08

La salud

Índice

Lección uno

Vocabulario 5
Clase 8
Diálogo 10
Examen 11
Respuestas 12

Lección dos

Vocabulario 17
Clase 19
Diálogo 22
Examen 23
Respuestas 24

Lección tres

Vocabulario 29
Clase 31
Diálogo 33
Examen 34
Respuestas 35

Lección cuatro

Vocabulario 41
Clase 43
Diálogo 45
Examen 46
Respuestas 47

Aprendamos viajando 53
Aprendamos conversando 59
Examen final 69

No se olvide de estudiar las lecciones en el manual antes de hacer los ejercicios de este cuaderno.

Examen inicial

Antes de comenzar el estudio de este volumen, dedique unos minutos a contestar a las 15 preguntas del examen siguiente. Llene el círculo correspondiente a la respuesta correcta.

1. *My shoulder _____.*
   O a) has a backache
   O b) is a pain
   O c) pains
   O d) aches
   O e) ache

2. *_____ his elbow _____?*
   O a) Why does, hurts
   O b) Why, aches
   O c) Do, aches
   O d) Do, ache
   O e) Does, hurt

3. *Do you _____ earache?*
   O a) hurt some
   O b) have an
   O c) have
   O d) have a
   O e) hurt an

4. *What's the _____?*
   O a) stomache
   O b) hurt
   O c) hurt
   O d) matter
   O e) wrong

5. *I have a __ throat and a ____.*
   O a) hurt, temperature
   O b) ache, temperature
   O c) sore, fever
   O d) sore, runny
   O e) fever, sore

6. *The pharmacist's _____ was very helpful.*
   O a) temperature

   O b) cold
   O c) prescribe
   O d) symptom
   O e) advice

7. *Those shoes hurt my feet. _____ wear them.*
   O a) I shouldn't
   O b) She should
   O c) I can
   O d) She can
   O e) I am

8. *You are _____ a lot. You should see the doctor.*
   O a) ache
   O b) fever
   O c) coughing
   O d) runny nose
   O e) sneeze

9. *Drink lots of___ rest and take two _____.*
   O a) orange juice, pill
   O b) coffee, medicines
   O c) fluids, aspirin
   O d) medicine, tablet
   O e) water, capsule

10. *Listening to the message on an answering machine _____ usually difficult.*
   O a) happened
   O b) is
   O c) shouldn't
   O d) has
   O e) happens

11. *To hear this _____ again, press the star key.*
   O a) appointments
   O b) reception
   O c) speaking
   O d) phone
   O e) message

12. *This medicine __ cause drowsiness.*
   O a) don't
   O b) is
   O c) wasn't
   O d) isn't
   O e) may

13. *___does the prescription have?*
   O a) When
   O b) How much
   O c) How many refills
   O d) How many
   O e) How possible

14. *Did the doctor __ you a prescription?*
   O a) give
   O b) mark
   O c) make
   O d) recommended
   O e) tell

15. *2 tsp. 3 X day _____*
   O a) Take three tablets daily.
   O b) Take 2 teaspoons at 3:00 each day.
   O c) Take two tablets twice a day.
   O d) Take 2 tablespoons three times a day.
   O e) Take 2 teaspoons three times a day.

Cuando haya estudiado todas las lecciones de este volumen, haga el mismo examen de nuevo. Lo encontrará al final de este cuaderno, en la página titulada "Examen final".

Compare los resultados obtenidos en este examen con los del examen final. Así comprobará lo que ha aprendido y podrá medir su progreso.

Cuando haya terminado este examen, empiece a estudiar la Lección uno.

Lección

Encontrará las respuestas en la página 12.

A. Resuelva el crucigrama.

Primero, complete las oraciones. Después, escriba las palabras que completan las oraciones en el cuadro siguiente, empezando por la casilla que lleva el número correspondiente.

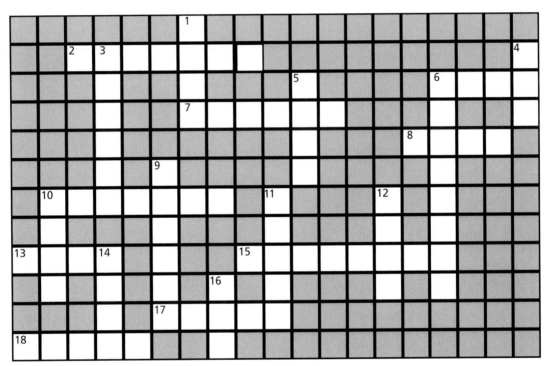

Horizontales

2.

7.

6. My arm hurts.
   It's very _____.

5

Encontrará las respuestas en la página 12.

8.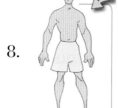

10. He is Dr. Martin's _____.

13.   She felt _____so she went home.

15.

17.

18.

Verticales

1.

3. He has a sore _____.

4.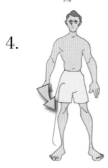

5.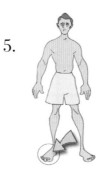

6.

9.   Take care of your _____.

10.   She has a _____in her arm.

11.

12.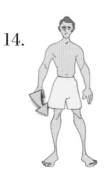

14.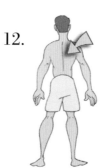

16.

Encontrará las respuestas en la página 12.

B. Delante de cada oración, escriba la letra del dibujo correspondiente.

a   b   c   d

e   f   g   h

Ejemplo: _e_   Her leg hurts.

1. _____   She has a backache.

2. _____   Their arms hurt.

3. _____   She has an earache.

4. _____   His head hurts.

5. _____   She has a stomachache.

6. _____   He has a pain in his neck.

7. _____   I think his toe hurts.

7

Encontrará las respuestas en la página 13.

**C. Complete las oraciones relacionadas con los dibujos.
En ciertos casos, hay más de una respuesta correcta.**

Ejemplo: He has a pain in his ____*knee*____.

1.   His knee _____.

2.   His _____ hurts.

3.   He has a _____ shoulder.

4.   His _____ aches.

5.   Does his elbow _____?

6.   The man _____ a sore throat.

7.   His neck _____, too.

8.   _____ chest aches.

9.   He has a _____ in his chest.

Encontrará las respuestas en la página 13.

D. Escriba las preguntas correspondientes a estas oraciones. Use las palabras entre paréntesis.

Ejemplo: He has a headache.

Does he have a headache?

1. Her stomach hurts.

    _____

2. Their shoulders ache.

    _____

3. She is sick.

    _____

4. The pain is in his knee.

    _____

5. My knee is sore.

    (you) _____

6. My wife has a stomachache.

    (you) _____

7. He hurt his arm yesterday.

    _____

8. I feel better today.

    (you) _____

Encontrará las respuestas en la página 14.

Elija la respuesta correcta.

1. Ángel   How are you today?
   Mario   Not too good.
         a) I feel great.
         b) I have a headache.

2. Julio   a) What's the matter?
         b) I don't feel well.
   Kim   Oh. You look fine.

3. Jim   I have a pain in my chest.
   Kathy   a) Does it hurt?
         b) Is it a sharp pain?

4. Lee   My leg hurts.
   Joseph   a) Is it your knee or your ankle?
         b) Is it your wrist or your elbow?

5. Barbara   Do you have a stomachache?
   Sam   a) No, the pain is in my chest.
         b) Yes, the pain is in my chest.

6. Terry   a) My wife is sick.
         b) I am ill.
   Nurse   Where is her pain?

Encontrará las respuestas en la página 14.

Llene los espacios en blanco con las palabras indicadas a continuación.

hurts	backache	pain	matter	sharp
ache	earache	ankle	feel	sore

Ejemplo: She has a __*backache*__.

1. My head _____.

2. She has an _____.

3. I have a _____ in my shoulder.

4. Is the pain in your knee or your _____?

5. Do you _____ OK?

6. It's a _____ pain.

7. My knees _____.

8. What's the _____?

9. Do you have a _____ throat?

Vocabulario

A.

Crossword puzzle:
- 1 Down: HEART (H)
- 2 Across: STOMACH
- 3 Down: THROAT
- 4 Down: LEG
- 5 Down: FOOT
- 6 Across: SORE
- 7 Across: DOCTOR
- 8 Across: BODY
- 9 Down: HAND
- 10 Across: PATIENT
- 10 Down: PAIN
- 11 Down: CHEST
- 12 Down: BACK
- 13 Across: SICK
- 14 Down: KNEE
- 15 Across: HEADACHE
- 16 Down: EYES
- 17 Across: HEART
- 18 Across: BONES

B.
1. d
2. h
3. g
4. a
5. b
6. f
7. c

Clase

C.
1. hurts (*or* aches)
2. shoulder
3. sore
4. elbow
5. hurt (*or* ache)
6. has
7. aches (*or* hurts)
8. His
9. pain

D.
1. Does her stomach hurt?
2. Do their shoulders ache?
3. Is she sick?
4. Is the pain in his knee? (*or* Does he have a pain in his knee?)
5. Is your knee sore?
6. Does your wife have a stomachache?
7. Did he hurt his arm yesterday?
8. Do you feel better today?

Diálogo

1. b
2. b
3. b
4. a
5. a
6. a

Examen

1. hurts
2. earache
3. pain
4. ankle
5. feel
6. sharp
7. ache
8. matter
9. sore

Lección

2

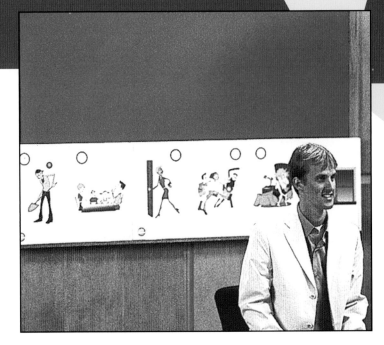

Encontrará las respuestas en la página 24.

A. Elija la palabra correcta.

Ejemplo: He has a (runny)/running nose.

1. Please take your fever/temperature.

2. Is your throat sore/hurt?

3. She is cough/coughing.

4. The advice/symptom was very helpful.

5. The pharmacy/pharmacist will answer your question.

6. That was a loud sneezing/sneeze.

7. Is your left arm numbness/numb?

8. I have some congestion/dizziness in my chest.

9. In the US, people use Celsius/Fahrenheit thermometers.

10. You should go home and rest/go home.

Encontrará las respuestas en la página 24.

B. Sopa de letras
Encuentre las palabras de la lista siguiente en el cuadro de abajo.
Tenga en cuenta que las palabras se leen de izquierda a derecha
y de arriba abajo.

advice, appointment, cold, cough, drugstore, fever, flu,
ill, pharmacy, rest, runny nose, should, sneeze, sore,
symptom, temperature, thermometer

T	E	M	P	E	R	A	T	U	R	E
H	H	A	H	S	M	P	F	L	U	U
E	T	R	A	Y	U	P	A	G	N	D
R	S	A	R	M	C	O	L	D	N	R
M	H	D	M	P	O	I	I	I	Y	U
O	O	V	A	T	A	N	F	L	N	G
M	U	I	C	O	H	T	E	L	O	S
E	L	C	Y	M	N	M	V	I	S	T
T	D	E	A	S	N	E	E	Z	E	O
E	C	O	U	G	H	N	R	G	Y	R
R	E	S	T	I	U	T	S	O	R	E

Encontrará las respuestas en la página 25.

C. Complete las oraciones con "should" o "shouldn't".

Ejemplo: She has a backache. She ___*shouldn't*___ lift that heavy box.

1. He has a cold. He _____ drink a lot of fluids.

2. His temperature is 98.6° He _____ worry.

3. You have a sharp pain in your chest. You _____ call the doctor now.

4. Those shoes hurt my feet. I _____ wear them.

5. She has a headache. She _____ take some aspirin.

6. They are too tired. They _____ work so hard.

7. He's a doctor. You _____ take his advice.

8. You _____ pick up that prescription today.

Encontrará las respuestas en la página 25.

D. Conteste a las preguntas relacionadas con los dibujos.

Ejemplo: What's the matter?

Mark is sneezing.

Is he coughing?

No, he's sneezing.

1.   Is he coughing?

_____

2.   Does he have a cough?

_____

Encontrará las respuestas en la página 25.

3. Is his nose running?

_____

4. Does he have a runny nose?

_____

5. Does he have an earache or a sore throat?

_____

6. How does he feel?

_____

7. Is he taking his temperature?

_____

8. Does he have a fever?

_____

Encontrará las respuestas en la página 26.

Llene los espacios en blanco.

Ken	_____, Maribel and Anna. How are _____?
Maribel	I feel great.
Anna	_____, too. How are you,_____?
Ken	_____ too good.
Maribel	_____ the matter?
Ken	I have _____ cold.
Anna	Does _____ throat hurt?
Ken	_____ little. I cough all the time.
Maribel	Do you have a _____?
Ken	I _____ know. I didn't_____ my temperature. Achoo!
Maribel	Oh, _____ you.
Ken	Thanks. I _____ a pain in my chest, too.
Maribel	Is _____ a sharp pain?
Ken	No. My chest aches. _____ whole body aches!
	And I have _____ earache!
Anna	Do you have a stomachache, _____?
Ken	No.
Anna	Sorry, I'm just kidding. You should_____ home _____ rest.
Maribel	That _____ like a good idea.
Ken	_____ does sound like a good idea.

Encontrará las respuestas en la página 26.

John está hablando con la enfermera. Ponga las oraciones de esta conversación en el orden correcto.

_____ What are your symptoms?

_____ I don't feel well.

_____ OK, thank you very much. Goodbye.

_____ No, it doesn't.

__*1*__ This is the nurse. How can I help you?

_____ A little. My temperature is 99.9°.

_____ Drink lots of fluids, rest and take two aspirin.
Call me tomorrow if you don't feel better.

_____ My head aches. I have a runny nose and my throat is sore.

_____ That's not too bad. Does it hurt when you breath?

_____ Do you have a fever?

Vocabulario

A.
1. temperature
2. sore
3. coughing
4. advice
5. pharmacist
6. sneeze
7. numb
8. congestion
9. Fahrenheit
10. rest

B.

T	E	M	P	E	R	A	T	U	R	E
H	H	A	H	S	M	P	F	L	U	U
E	T	R	A	Y	U	P	A	G	N	D
R	S	A	R	M	C	O	L	D	N	R
M	H	D	M	P	O	I	I	I	Y	U
O	O	V	A	T	A	N	F	L	N	G
M	U	I	C	O	H	T	E	L	O	S
E	L	C	Y	M	N	M	V	I	S	T
T	D	E	A	S	N	E	E	Z	E	O
E	C	O	U	G	H	N	R	G	Y	R
R	E	S	T	I	U	T	S	O	R	E

Clase

C.
1. should
2. shouldn't
3. should
4. shouldn't
5. should
6. shouldn't
7. should
8. should

D.
1. Yes, he is.
2. Yes, he does.
3. Yes, it is.
4. Yes, he does.
5. He has a sore throat.
6. He feels terrible.
7. Yes, he is.
8. Yes, he does./No, he doesn't./I don't know.

Respuestas

Diálogo

Ken	<u>Hi</u>, Maribel and Anna. How are <u>you</u>?
Maribel	I feel great.
Anna	<u>Me</u>, too. How are you, <u>Ken</u>?
Ken	<u>Not</u> too good.
Maribel	<u>What's</u> the matter?
Ken	I have <u>a</u> cold.
Anna	Does <u>your</u> throat hurt?
Ken	<u>A</u> little. I cough all the time.
Maribel	Do you have a <u>fever</u>?
Ken	I <u>don't</u> know. I didn't <u>take</u> my temperature. Achoo!
Maribel	Oh, <u>bless</u> you.
Ken	Thanks. I <u>have</u> a pain in my chest, too.
Maribel	Is <u>it</u> a sharp pain?
Ken	No. My chest aches. <u>My</u> whole body aches! And I have <u>an</u> earache!
Anna	Do you have a stomachache, <u>too</u>?
Ken	No.
Anna	Sorry, I'm just kidding. You should <u>go</u> home <u>and</u> rest.
Maribel	That <u>sounds</u> like a good idea.
Ken	<u>That</u> (or <u>It</u>) does sound like a good idea.

Examen

__3__ What are your symptoms?

__2__ I don't feel well.

__10__ OK, thank you very much. Goodbye.

__8__ No, it doesn't.

__1__ This is the nurse. How can I help you?

__6__ A little. My temperature is 99.9°.

__9__ Drink lots of fluids, rest and take two aspirin.
Call me tomorrow if you don't feel better.

__4__ My head aches. I have a runny nose and my throat is sore.

__7__ That's not too bad. Does it hurt when you breath?

__5__ Do you have a fever?

Lección

3

Inglés sin Barreras

Encontrará las respuestas en la página 35.

A. Relacione cada número, símbolo o expresión con una de las categorías siguientes.

~~key pad~~	medical insurance identification number
telephone number	appointment time	medical center address

Ejemplo: # _____*key pad*_____

1. 0 _____

2. 555-1299 _____

3. 10:30, Tuesday _____

4. 2298GG3 _____

5. 449 Oak Street _____

6. (310) 555-3333 _____

7. * _____

8. 895 Main _____

9. 2:00 PM _____

10. ID#342-88-12 _____

Encontrará las respuestas en la página 35.

B. Ponga las letras en orden. Ya está colocada la primera letra.

1. eessnorp   r_____

2. eoaoprtr   o_____

3. gessmae   m _____

4. yombls   s_____

5. ntxameiaoni   e_____

6. toppmnetain   a_____

7. aaalebvil   a_____

8. preceisttnio   r_____

Encontrará las respuestas en la página 36.

C. Lea el correo electrónico que Gonzalo envió a su amiga Maritza y luego conteste a las preguntas.

Maritza. How are you doing? I was sick last week. I had the flu, I think. After two days, I called my doctor's office to make an appointment. It was about 7:00 PM. When I heard the voice on the phone, I started to talk. But the voice just kept talking, telling me to press different numbers. It was an answering machine!

I couldn't understand anything. I listened to the whole message and then I hung up the phone and went to bed. I stayed in bed for two more days.

I didn't go to the doctor but I feel better now. Next time I'll be ready for the answering machine. Best, Gonzalo

1. When was Gonzalo sick?

   _____

2. What was wrong with him?

   _____

3. What time did Gonzalo call the doctor?

   _____

4. Who answered the phone?

   _____

5. Did Gonzalo make an appointment?

   _____

6. How does Gonzalo feel now?

   _____

Encontrará las respuestas en la página 36.

D. Lea la respuesta de Maritza. Haga un círculo alrededor de la palabra correcta.

Dear Gonzalo,

I'm glad you 1. (are/were) better now. Listening to the message on an

answering machine 2. (is/was) usually difficult. Sometimes you 3. (could/can)

listen to the message again. At the end of the message, the voice 4. (will/is)

give you directions. It will say something like, 5. "(Pressing/Press) 1 to listen

to the message again." Then you can listen to the message again and again—until

you 6. (understand/understood) it! This 7. (happened/happens) to me almost

every week. Take care and I 8. (will not/will) call you next week.

Your friend, Maritza

Encontrará las respuestas en la página 37.

Dibuje una línea que una la pregunta de la recepcionista con la respuesta correspondiente.

Receptionist	Patient
How can I help you?	It's 100.2°.
What are your symptoms?	Excuse me. Did you say 2:15 or 2:50?
What is your temperature?	It's 4670AK2.
Would you like to make an appointment?	I have a fever and a sore throat.
Can you come this afternoon at 2:50?	I don't feel well.
2:50. What is your insurance number?	Yes, please.

Encontrará las respuestas en la página 37.

Lea el mensaje grabado en el contestador automático. Luego, lea las oraciones y decida qué tecla se tiene que pulsar en cada caso.

Thank you for calling Dr. King's office. To hear this message in Spanish, press 2. To leave a message for the receptionist, press 3. To leave a message for the nurse, press 4. If you'd like to make or confirm an appointment, press 3. To schedule tests, please press 4. To leave a private message for Dr. King, press 5. If this is an emergency, dial 911. To hear this message again, press the star key.

Ejemplo: Juan doesn't speak English. ___*press 2*___

1. Maryanne wants to leave a message for the doctor. _____

2. Joe wants to confirm his appointment. _____

3. Elizabeth needs an X-ray. _____

4. Mr. Topp cut his finger very badly. _____

5. Julie didn't understand the message. _____

6. Mariah wants to leave a message for the nurse. _____

Vocabulario

A.
1. key pad
2. telephone number
3. appointment time
4. medical insurance identification number
5. medical center address
6. telephone number
7. key pad
8. medical center address
9. appointment time
10. medical insurance identification number

B.
1. response
2. operator
3. message
4. symbol
5. examination
6. appointment
7. available
8. receptionist

Clase

C.
1. He was sick last week.
2. He thinks he had the flu.
3. He called the doctor at about 7:00 PM.
4. An answering machine answered the phone.
5. No, Gonzalo didn't make an appointment.
6. He feels better.

D.
1. are
2. is
3. can
4. will
5. Press
6. understand
7. happens
8. will

Diálogo

Receptionist	Patient
How can I help you?	I don't feel well.
What are your symptoms?	I have a fever and a sore throat.
What is your temperature?	It's 100.2°.
Would you like to make an appointment?	Yes, please.
Can you come this afternoon at 2:50?	Excuse me. Did you say 2:15 or 2:50?
2:50. What is your insurance number?	It's 4670AK2.

Examen

1. press 5
2. press 3
3. press 4
4. dial 911
5. press the star key
6. press 4

Lección 4

Inglés sin Barreras

Encontrará las respuestas en la página 47.

A. Sopa de letras

Encuentre las palabras de la lista siguiente en el cuadro de abajo. Tenga en cuenta que las palabras se leen de izquierda a derecha y de arriba abajo.

bottle, capsule, cause, dosage, empty, exactly,
full, label, liquid, medication, once, pill, possible,
powder, prescribe, refill, tablet, twice

M	E	D	I	C	A	T	I	O	N	F	P
P	X	O	N	C	E	A	H	O	E	U	A
R	A	S	L	A	C	B	O	T	T	L	E
E	C	A	I	U	E	L	E	W	E	L	M
S	T	G	Q	S	R	E	F	I	L	L	P
C	L	E	U	E	L	T	T	C	I	A	T
R	Y	P	I	L	L	D	F	E	L	B	Y
I	W	E	D	C	A	P	S	U	L	E	T
B	K	P	O	W	D	E	R	S	N	L	S
E	P	O	S	S	I	B	L	E	R	T	E

Vocabulario

Encontrará las respuestas en la página 47.

B. Haga un círculo alrededor de la palabra correcta.

Ejemplo: Be sure to make/take an appointment.

1. This medicine should/may cause drowsiness.

2. Did you take/give his temperature?

3. How many symptoms/refills does the prescription have?

4. Did the doctor give/take you a prescription?

5. The nurse asked/told me what my symptoms were.

6. Make sure you take/make the correct dose.

7. The label says to take one tablet each/once morning.

8. The possible/recommended dosage is one tablespoon daily.

C. Relacione cada oración con su abreviatura correspondiente.

2 tsp. 3 X day	3 tabs. daily	1 tbsp. 2 X day
2 caps. 2 X day	1 tsp. w/ food	1 tsp. on empty stomach
1 cap. in AM	2 tabs. 2 X day	1 tbsp. as needed

Ejemplo: Take 2 teaspoons three times a day. *2 tsp, 3 X day*

1.   Take one tablespoon twice a day. _____

2.   Take one capsule in the morning. _____

3.   Take three tablets daily. _____

4.   Take two tablets twice a day. _____

5.   Take one teaspoon on an empty stomach. _____

6.   Take two capsules twice a day. _____

7.   Take one tablespoon as needed. _____

8.   Take one teaspoon with food. _____

Encontrará las respuestas en la página 48.

D. Ponga la letra correspondiente a cada instrucción en la columna correcta.

    a.   Do not mix with milk or milk products.

    b.   Caution: may cause drowsiness.

    c.   Take as needed.

    d.   Take with lots of water.

    e.   Take three tablespoons daily.

    f.   Take every evening.

    g.   Take all the pills.

    h.   Take in the morning.

    i.   No refills.

    j.   Do not exceed recommended dosage.

    k.   #1442900J

    l.   Take before bed.

When?	How much?	How?	Other
_____	_____	_a_	_____
_____	_____	_____	_____
_____	_____	_____	_____
_____	_____	_____	_____

Encontrará las respuestas en la página 48.

Elija la oración que corresponde con las instrucciones.

1. Caution: May cause drowsiness.

    a) Don't take the medicine and drive.

    b) Take the medicine before you leave for work.

2. Take on an empty stomach.

    a) Don't take on a full stomach.

    b) Be sure to eat before you take the medicine.

3. Take before bed.

    a) Any time before noon is good.

    b) Take it just before you go to sleep.

4. Do not mix with other antibiotics.

    a) Do not take any aspirin.

    b) Tell your doctor if you are taking other antibiotics.

5. Do not take if you have a fever.

    a) Take your temperature first.

    b) If you have a fever, take this medicine.

6. Two tablespoons each morning for seven days.

    a) There are no refills for this prescription.

    b) You'll need a spoon to take the medicine.

Encontrará las respuestas en la página 49.

Lea la etiqueta. Luego, conteste a las preguntas.

Beverly Medical Pharmacy
8770 Beverly
LA, CA   310-555-9990
3422950
Dr. H. Wu

James Smith   8/24
Cozzard 100 MG Tab   #30
Take one tablet daily.
Take on an empty stomach.
Refills: 3

1. Who is the patient?

2. What is the name of the doctor?

3. What is the prescription number?

4. What is the name of the pharmacy?

5. What is the name of the medicine?

6. What is the dosage?

7. Are there any cautions?

8. How many refills are there?

Vocabulario

A.

```
M E D I C A T I O N F P
P X O N C E A H O E U A
R A S L A C B O T T L E
E C A I U E L E W E L M
S T G Q S R E F I L L P
C L E U E L T T C I A T
R Y P I L L D F E L B Y
I W E D C A P S U L E T
B K P O W D E R S N L S
E P O S S I B L E R T E
```

B.
1. may
2. take
3. refills
4. give
5. asked
6. take
7. each
8. recommended

Clase

C.
1. 1 tbsp. 2 X day
2. 1 cap. in AM
3. 3 tabs. daily
4. 2 tabs. 2 X day
5. 1 tsp. on empty stomach
6. 2 caps. 2 X day
7. 1 tbsp. as needed
8. 1 tsp. w/food

D. When?   <u>c, f, h, l</u>

How much? <u>e, g, j</u>

How?   <u>a, d</u>

Other   <u>b, i, k</u>

Diálogo

1. a)
2. a)
3. b)
4. b)
5. a)
6. b)

Examen

1. James Smith.
2. Dr. H. Wu.
3. # 3422950.
4. Beverly Medical Pharmacy.
5. Cozzard.
6. One tablet daily. *or* 100 MG daily.
7. Yes. Take on an empty stomach.
8. Three.

Aprendamos viajando

V

Boston

Antes de completar este ejercicio, vea la sección "Aprendamos viajando" incluida en el video y lea la misma sección en el manual.

Si la información contenida en la oración es verdadera, haga un círculo alrededor de la palabra **True**. Si la información es falsa, haga un círculo alrededor de la palabra **False** y escriba una oración con la información correcta.

True   *False*   1. Boston is in Massachusetts.

_____

True   *False*   2. Many events related to the Revolutionary War took place in Boston.

_____

True   *False*   3. It is called "Europe's American City."

_____

True   *False*   4. The Freedom Train is a tour of historic sites.

_____

True   *False*   5. Paul Revere began his midnight ride at the Old North Church.

_____

True   False   6. The Boston Coffee Party was a famous event.

_____

True   False   7. Faneuil Hall is called the "Cradle of Liberty."

_____

True   False   8. Italian is spoken on the streets of the North End.

_____

True   False   9. The New England Aquarium is on East Wharf.

_____

True   False   10. Harvard and MIT are in Cambridge.

_____

True   False   11. Harvard is called an Ivy Tree school.

_____

True   False   12. MIT is known for its scientific research.

_____

1. True.
2. True.
3. False. It is called "America's European City."
4. False. The Freedom Trail is a tour of historic sites.
5. True.
6. False. The Boston Tea Party was a famous event.
7. True.
8. True.
9. False. It's on Central Wharf.
10. True.
11. False. Harvard is an Ivy League school.
12. True.

Notas

Aprendamos conversando

C Notas

Encontrará las respuestas en la página 64.

Actividad 1. Molestias y quejas: problemas de la salud
Escuche y repita.

Actividad 2. Alternativas: ¿Te sientes mal?
Escuche y repita.

Actividad 3. Formas alternativas: ¿Dónde te duele?
Escuche y describa qué molestias tiene usted.

Actividad 4. Prescripciones: formas alternativas
Escuche y marque con un círculo la forma alternativa de las oraciones que escuche.

1. Take one pill twice a day.

   Take two pills once a day.

2. Take two capsules once a day.

   Take two capsules twice a day.

3. Take three tablets once a day.

   Take one tablet three times per day.

4. Take one teaspoon twice a day.

   Take one teaspoon once a day.

5. Take one tablespoon three times a day.

   Take one teaspoon three times a day.

Encontrará las respuestas en la página 64.

Actividad 5. Diálogos
Escuche y conteste las preguntas que siguen.

Diálogo 1

Does Bill's knee hurt? _____

Diálogo 2

Does Ann have a sore throat? _____

Diálogo 3

Can Leslie see the doctor at one o'clock?_____

Diálogo 4

Should Dan take the tablets before or after he eats?

_____

Actividad 6. Síntomas: formas alternativas con "for" y "since"
Escuche y repita las preguntas y respuestas.
Luego, diga cada respuesta de una manera diferente.

How long have you_____?
I've _____ for _____.
I've _____ since _____ ago.

Aprendamos conversando

en la página 64.

Actividad 7. Consejos con el verbo auxiliar "should"
Escuche y marque con un círculo la respuesta más lógica.

1. You should go to sleep.
   You should exercise now.
2. You should go to work.
   You should see a doctor.
3. You should eat more.
   You should take an aspirin.
4. You should take a vacation.
   You should work more.
5. You should get a massage.
   You should carry these boxes.
6. You should go outside.
   You should take your temperature.
7. You should get a new prescription.
   You should take a pill.
8. You should run in the park now.
   You should sit down.
9. You should make an appointment.
   You should have a sore throat.
10. You should go to the dentist.
    You should eat some candy.

Encontrará las respuestas en la página 65.

Actividad 8. Pronunciación: "should" y "shouldn't"
Escuche, repita y marque "should" o "shouldn't" con un
círculo para indicar si la oración es positiva o negativa.

1. should   shouldn't

2. should   shouldn't

3. should   shouldn't

4. should   shouldn't

5. should   shouldn't

6. should   shouldn't

7. should   shouldn't

8. should   shouldn't

9. should   shouldn't

10. should   shouldn't

Actividad 9. Consejos: formas alternativas
Escuche y repita.

You should...

You ought to...

Take my advice and...

I suggest that you...

I recommend that you...

You might want to...

Aprendamos conversando

Encontrará las respuestas en la página 65.

Actividad 10. Scarborough Fair: formas alternativas
Escuche y escriba estas frases y sus formas alternativas.

a true love of mine   <u>one of my true loves</u>

a friend of mine   _____

a teacher of mine   _____

a problem of mine   _____

a cousin of mine   _____

a favorite song of mine   _____

Actividad 11. Scarborough Fair: hierbas medicinales
Conteste a las preguntas de acuerdo con la información del cuadro siguiente.

	upset stomach	insect bites	headache	dandruff	congestion	sore throat	bronchitis
parsley	√	√					
sage	√					√	
rosemary	√		√	√	√		
thyme	√						√

Note: This is an English practice activity only and is not intended to suggest treatment of a health problem or as a substitute for consulting a licensed medical professional.

Nota: Ésta es sólamente una actividad de práctica del idioma inglés y no tiene la intención de sugerir un tratamiento para problemas de la salud o sustituir consultas con el médico o personal médico certificado.

C Respuestas

Actividad 4.

1. ~~Take one pill twice a day~~
   Take two pills once a day.
2. ~~Take two capsules once a day~~
   Take two capsules twice a day.
3. Take three tablets once a day.
   ~~Take one tablet three times per day~~
4. Take one teaspoon twice a day.
   ~~Take one teaspoon once a day~~
5. ~~Take one tablespoon three times a day~~
   Take one teaspoon three times a day.

Actividad 5.

Diálogo 1
Does Bill's knee hurt? Yes, it does.
Diálogo 2
Does Ann have a sore throat? No, she doesn't.
Diálogo 3
Can Leslie see the doctor at one o'clock? No, she can't.
Diálogo 4
Should Dan take the tablets before or after he eats?
He should take them after he eats.

Actividad 7.

1. ~~You should go to sleep~~
   You should exercise now.
2. You should go to work.
   ~~You should see a doctor~~
3. You should eat more.
   ~~You should take an aspirin~~
4. ~~You should take a vacation~~
   You should work more.
5. ~~You should get a massage~~
   You should carry these boxes.

6. You should go outside.
    ~~You should take your temperature~~.
7. ~~You should get a new prescription~~.
    You should take a pill.
8. You should run in the park now.
    ~~You should sit down~~.
9. ~~You should make an appointment~~.
    You should have a sore throat.
10. ~~You should go to the dentist~~.
    You should eat some candy.

Actividad 8.

1. **should** shouldn't
2. should **shouldn't**
3. should **shouldn't**
4. **should** shouldn't
5. **should** shouldn't
6. should **shouldn't**
7. should **shouldn't**
8. **should** shouldn't
9. should **shouldn't**
10. **should** shouldn't

Actividad 10.

a true love of mine	one of my true loves
a friend of mine	one of my friends
a teacher of mine	one of my teachers
a problem of mine	one of my problems
a cousin of mine	one of my cousins
a favorite song of mine	one of my favorite songs

Notas

Notas

Notas

68

Examen final 8

Llene el círculo correspondiente a la respuesta correcta.

1. *My shoulder* _____.
   - ○ a) has a backache
   - ○ b) is a pain
   - ○ c) pains
   - ○ d) aches
   - ○ e) ache

2. _____ *his elbow* _____?
   - ○ a) Why does, hurts
   - ○ b) Why, aches
   - ○ c) Do, aches
   - ○ d) Do, ache
   - ○ e) Does, hurt

3. *Do you* _____ *earache?*
   - ○ a) hurt some
   - ○ b) have an
   - ○ c) have
   - ○ d) have a
   - ○ e) hurt an

4. *What's the* _____?
   - ○ a) stomache
   - ○ b) hurt
   - ○ c) hurt
   - ○ d) matter
   - ○ e) wrong

5. *I have a __ throat and a ____.*
   - ○ a) hurt, temperature
   - ○ b) ache, temperature
   - ○ c) sore, fever
   - ○ d) sore, runny
   - ○ e) fever, sore

6. *The pharmacist's _____ was very helpful.*
   - ○ a) temperature
   - ○ b) cold

   - ○ c) prescribe
   - ○ d) symptom
   - ○ e) advice

7. *Those shoes hurt my feet. _____ wear them.*
   - ○ a) I shouldn't
   - ○ b) She should
   - ○ c) I can
   - ○ d) She can
   - ○ e) I am

8. *You are _____ a lot. You should see the doctor.*
   - ○ a) ache
   - ○ b) fever
   - ○ c) coughing
   - ○ d) runny nose
   - ○ e) sneeze

9. *Drink lots of___ rest and take two _____.*
   - ○ a) orange juice, pill
   - ○ b) coffee, medicines
   - ○ c) fluids, aspirin
   - ○ d) medicine, tablet
   - ○ e) water, capsule

10. *Listening to the message on an answering machine _____ usually difficult.*
    - ○ a) happened
    - ○ b) is
    - ○ c) shouldn't
    - ○ d) has
    - ○ e) happens

11. *To hear this _____ again, press the star key.*
    - ○ a) appointments
    - ○ b) reception
    - ○ c) speaking
    - ○ d) phone
    - ○ e) message

12. *This medicine __ cause drowsiness.*
    - ○ a) don't
    - ○ b) is
    - ○ c) wasn't
    - ○ d) isn't
    - ○ e) may

13. *___does the prescription have?*
    - ○ a) When
    - ○ b) How much
    - ○ c) How many refills
    - ○ d) How many
    - ○ e) How possible

14. *Did the doctor __ you a prescription?*
    - ○ a) give
    - ○ b) mark
    - ○ c) make
    - ○ d) recommended
    - ○ e) tell

15. *2 tsp. 3 X day _____*
    - ○ a) Take three tablets daily.
    - ○ b) Take 2 teaspoons at 3:00 each day.
    - ○ c) Take two tablets twice a day.
    - ○ d) Take 2 tablespoons three times a day.
    - ○ e) Take 2 teaspoons three times a day.